Poems of Optimism

Ella Wheeler Wilcox

Contents

GREATER BRITAIN	7
BELGIUM	8
KNITTING	8
MOBILISATION	10
NEUTRAL	11
A BOOK FOR THE KING	11
THE MEN-MADE GODS	12
THE GHOSTS	13
THE POET'S THEME	14
EUROPE	16
AFTER	17
THE PEACE ANGEL	17
PEACE SHOULD NOT COME	18
THE WINDS OF FATE	19
BEAUTY	20
THE INVISIBLE HELPERS	22
TO THE WOMEN OF AUSTRALIA	23
REPLIES	24
EARTH BOUND	25
A SUCCESSFUL MAN	27
UNSATISFIED	28
EPARATION	30
TO THE TEACHERS OF THE YOUNG	33
BEAUTY MAKING	33
ON AVON'S BREAST I SAW A STATELY SWAN	34
THE LITTLE GO-CART	35
I AM RUNNING FORTH TO MEET YOU	36
MARTYRS OF PEACE	37
HOME	38
THE ETERNAL NOW	40
IF I WERE A MAN, A YOUNG MAN	40
WE MUST SEND THEM OUT TO PLAY	42
PROTEST	43
REWARD	44
THIS IS MY TASK	44
THE STATUE	46
BEHOLD THE EARTH	47

WHAT THEY SAW	48
HIS LAST LETTER	50
A WISH	55
JUSTICE	56
AN OLD SONG	57
OH, POOR, SICK WORLD	58
PRAISE DAY	60
INTERLUDE	61
THE LAND OF THE GONE-AWAY-SOULS	62
THE HARP'S SONG	63
THE PENDULUM	64
AN OLD-FASHIONED TYPE	65
THE SWORD	67
LOVE AND THE SEASONS	68
A NAUGHTY LITTLE COMET	70
THE LAST DANCE	71
WHEN LOVE FOR HIS MAKER AWOKE IN MAN, THE DANCE BEGAN	71
A VAGABOND MIND	72
MY FLOWER ROOM	73
MY FAITH	75
ARROW AND BOW	76
IF WE SHOULD MEET HIM	79
FAITH	80
THE SECRET OF PRAYER	81
THE ANSWER	82
A VISION	83
THE SECOND COMING	85

POEMS OF OPTIMISM

BY

Ella Wheeler Wilcox

GREATER BRITAIN

Our hearts were not set on fighting,
   We did not pant for the fray,
And whatever wrongs need righting,
   We would not have met that way.
But the way that has opened before us
   Leads on thro' a blood-red field;
And we swear by the great God o'er us,
   We will die, but we will not yield.

The battle is not of our making,
   And war was never our plan;
Yet, all that is sweet forsaking,
   We march to it, man by man.
It is either to smite, or be smitten,
   There's no other choice to-day;
And we live, as befits the Briton,
   Or we die, as the Briton may.

We were not fashioned for cages,
   Or to feed from a keeper's hand;
Our strength which has grown thro' ages
   Is the strength of a slave-free land.
We cannot kneel down to a master,

    To our God alone can we pray;
And we stand in this world disaster,
    To fight, like a lion at bay.

BELGIUM

Ruined? destroyed? Ah, no; though blood in rivers ran
Down all her ancient streets; though treasures manifold
Love-wrought, Time-mellowed, and beyond the price of gold
Are lost, yet Belgium's star shines still in God's vast plan.

Rarely have Kings been great, since kingdoms first began;
Rarely have great kings been great men, when all was told.
But, by the lighted torch in mailed hands, behold,
Immortal Belgium's immortal king, and Man.

KNITTING

At the concert and the play
Everywhere you see them sitting,
Knitting, knitting.
Women who the other day
Thought of nothing but their frocks

Or their jewels or their locks,
Women who have lived for pleasure,
Who have known no work but leisure,
Now are knitting, knitting, knitting
For the soldiers over there.

On the trains and on the ships
With a diligence befitting,
They are knitting.
Some with smiles upon their lips,
Some with manners debonair,
Some with earnest look and air.
But each heart in its own fashion,
Weaves in pity and compassion
In their knitting, knitting, knitting
For the soldiers over there.

Hurried women to and fro
From their homes to labour flitting,
Knitting, knitting,
Busy handed come and go.
Broken bits of time they spare,
Just to feel they do their share,
Just to keep life's sense of beauty
In the doing of a duty,
They are knitting, knitting, knitting
For the soldiers over there.

MOBILISATION

Oh the Kings of earth have mobilised their men.
See them moving, valour proving,
To the fields of glory going,
Banners flowing, bugles blowing,
Every one a mother's son,
Brave with uniform and gun,
Keeping step with easy swing,
Yes, with easy step and light marching onward to the fight,
Just to please the warlike fancy of a King;
Who has mobilised his army for the strife.

Oh the King of Death has mobilised his men.
See the hearses huge and black
How they rumble down the track;
With their coffins filled with dead,
Filled with men who fought and bled;
Now from fields of glory coming
To the sound of muffled drumming
They are lying still and white,
But the Kings have had their fight;
Death has mobilised his army for the grave.

NEUTRAL

That pale word 'Neutral' sits becomingly
On lips of weaklings. But the men whose brains
Find fuel in their blood, the men whose minds
Hold sympathetic converse with their hearts,
Such men are never neutral. That word stands
Unsexed and impotent in Realms of Speech.
When mighty problems face a startled world
No virile man is neutral. Right or wrong
His thoughts go forth, assertive, unafraid
To stand by his convictions, and to do
Their part in shaping issues to an end.
Silence may guard the door of useless words,
At dictate of Discretion; but to stand
Without opinions in a world which needs
Constructive thinking, is a coward's part.

A BOOK FOR THE KING

A book has been made for the King,
A book of beauty and art;
To the good king's eyes
A smile shall rise
Hiding the ache in his heart -

Hiding the hurt and the grief
As he turns it, leaf by leaf.

A book has been made for the King,
A book of blood and of blight;
To the Great King's eyes
A look shall rise
That will blast and wither and smite -
Yes, smite with a just God's rage,
As He turns it, page by page.

THE MEN-MADE GODS

Said the Kaiser's god to the god of the Czar:
   'Hark, hark, how my people pray.
Their faith, methinks, is greater by far
Than all the faiths of the others are;
   They know I will help them slay.'

Said the god of the Czar: 'My people call
   In a medley of tongues; they know
I will lend my strength to them one and all.
Wherever they fight their foes shall fall
   Like grass where the mowers go.'

Then the god of the Gauls spoke out of a cloud
   To the god of the King nearby:
'Our people pray, tho' they pray not loud;
They ask for courage to slaughter a crowd,

And to laugh, tho' themselves may die.'

And far out into the heart of Space
   Where a lonely pathway crept,
Up over the stars, to a secret place,
Where no light shone but the light of His face,
   Christ covered His eyes and wept.

THE GHOSTS

There was no wind, and yet the air
   Seemed suddenly astir;
There were no forms, and yet all space
   Seemed thronged with growing hosts.
They came from Where, and from Nowhere,
   Like phantoms as they were;
They came from many a land and place -
   The ghosts, the ghosts, the ghosts.

And some were white, and some were grey,
   And some were red as blood -
Those ghosts of men who met their death
   Upon the field of war.
Against the skies of fading day,
   Like banks of cloud they stood;
And each wraith asked another wraith,
   'What were we fighting for?'

One said, 'I was my mother's all;

    And she was old and blind.'
Another, 'Back on earth, my wife
    And week-old baby lie.'
Another, 'At the bugle's call,
    I left my bride behind;
Love made so beautiful my life
    I could not bear to die.'

In voices like the winds that moan
    Among pine trees at night,
They whispered long, the newly dead,
    While listening stars came out.
'We wonder if the cause is known,
    And if the war was right,
That killed us in our prime,' they said,
    'And what it was about.'

They came in throngs that filled all space -
    Those whispering phantom hosts;
They came from many a land and place,
    The ghosts, the ghosts, the ghosts.

THE POET'S THEME

Why should the poet of these pregnant times
Be asked to sing of war's unholy crimes?

To laud and eulogise the trade which thrives
On horrid holocausts of human lives?

Man was a fighting beast when earth was young,
And war the only theme when Homer sung.

'Twixt might and might the equal contest lay:
Not so the battles of our modern day.

Too often now the conquering hero struts,
A Gulliver among the Lilliputs.

Success no longer rests on skill or fate,
But on the movements of a syndicate.

Of old, men fought and deemed it right and just,
To-day the warrior fights because he must;

And in his secret soul feels shame because
He desecrates the higher manhood's laws.

Oh, there are worthier themes for poet's pen
In this great hour than bloody deeds of men:

The rights of many--not the worth of one -
The coming issues, not the battle done;

The awful opulence and awful need -
The rise of brotherhood--the fall of greed;

The soul of man replete with God's own force,
The call 'to heights,' and not the cry 'to horse.'

Are there not better themes in this great age
For pen of poet, or for voice of sage,

Than those old tales of killing? Song is dumb
Only that greater song in time may come.

When comes the bard, he whom the world waits for,
He will not sing of War.

EUROPE

Little lads and grandsires,
Women old with care;
But all the men are dying men
Or dead men over there.

No one stops to dig graves;
Who has time to spare?
The dead men, the dead men
How the dead men stare.

Kings are out a-hunting -
Oh, the sport is rare;
With dying men and dead men
Falling everywhere.

Life for lads and grandsires;
Spoils for kings to share;
And dead men, dead men,
Dead men everywhere.

AFTER

Over the din of battle,
Over the cannons' rattle,
Over the strident voices of men and their dying groans,
I hear the falling of thrones.

Out of the wild disorder
That spreads from border to border,
I see a new world rising from ashes of ancient towns;
And the Rulers wear no crowns.

Over the blood-charged water,
Over the fields of slaughter,
Down to the hidden vaults of Time, where lie the worn-out things
I see the passing of Kings.

THE PEACE ANGEL

Angel of Peace, the hounds of war,
Unleashed, are all abroad,
And war's foul trade again is made
  Man's leading aim in life.
Blood dyes the billow and the sod;
  The very winds are rife

With tales of slaughter. Angel, pray,
What can we do or think or say
In times like these?
    'Child, think of God!'

'Before this little speck in space
Called Earth with light was shod,
Great chains and tiers of splendid spheres
   Were fashioned by His hand.
Be thine the part to love and laud,
   Nor seek to understand.
Go lift thine eyes from death-charged guns
To one who made a billion suns;
And trust and wait.
    Child, dwell on God!'

PEACE SHOULD NOT COME

Peace should not come along this foul, earth way.
Peace should not come, until we cleanse the path.
God waited for us; now in awful wrath
He pours the blood of men out day by day
To purify the highroad for her feet.
Why, what would Peace do, in a world where hearts
Are filled with thoughts like poison-pointed darts?
It were not meet, surely it were not meet
For Peace to come, and with her white robes hide
These industries of death--these guns and swords, -
These uniformed, hate-filled, destructive hordes, -

These hideous things, that are each nation's pride.
So long as men believe in armed might
Let arms be brandished. Let not Peace be sought
Until the race-heart empties out all thought
Of blows and blood, as arguments for Right.
The world has never had enough of war,
Else war were not. Now let the monster stand,
Until he slays himself with his own hand;
Though no man knows what he is fighting for.
Then in the place where wicked cannons stood
Let Peace erect her shrine of Brotherhood.

THE WINDS OF FATE

One ship drives east and another drives west,
With the self-same winds that blow,
  'Tis the set of the sails
  And not the gales
That tell them the way to go.
Like the winds of the sea are the winds of fate,
As we voyage along through life,
  'Tis the set of the soul
  That decides its goal
And not the calm or the strife.

BEAUTY

The search for beauty is the search for God
Who is All Beauty. He who seeks shall find.
And all along the paths my feet have trod,
I have sought hungrily with heart and mind,
   And open eyes for beauty, everywhere.
   Lo! I have found the world is very fair.
The search for beauty is the search for God.

Beauty was first revealed to me by stars,
   Before I saw it in my mother's eyes,
Or, seeing, sensed it beauty, I was stirred
To awe and wonder by those orbs of light
   All palpitant against empurpled skies.
They spoke a language to my childish heart
Of mystery and splendour, and of space,
Friendly with gracious, unseen presences.
Beauty was first revealed to me by stars.

Sunsets enlarged the meaning of the word.
   There was a window looking to the west;
Beyond it, wide Wisconsin fields of grain,
And then a hill, whereon white flocks of clouds
   Would gather in the afternoon to rest.
And when the sun went down behind that hill
What scenes of glory spread before my sight;
What beauty--beauty, absolute, supreme!
Sunsets enlarged the meaning of that word.

Clover in blossom, red and honey-sweet,
   In summer billowed like a crimson sea
Across the meadow lands. One day, I stood
Breast-high amidst its waves, and heard the hum
   Of myriad bees, that had gone mad like me
With fragrance and with beauty. Over us,
A loving sun smiled from a cloudless sky,
While a bold breeze kissed lightly as it passed,
Clover in blossom, red and honey-sweet.

Autumn spoke loudly of the beautiful.
   And in the gallery of Nature hung
Colossal pictures hard against the sky,
Set forests gorgeous with a hundred hues;
   And with each morning, some new wonder flung
Before the startled world; some daring shade,
Some strange, new scheme of colour and of form.
Autumn spoke loudly of the beautiful.

Winter, though rude, is delicate in art -
   More delicate than Summer or than fall
(Even as rugged man is more refined
In vital things than woman). Winter's touch
   On Nature seemed most beautiful of all -
That evanescent beauty of the frost
On window panes; of clean, fresh, fallen snow;
Of white, white sunlight on the ice-draped trees.
Winter, though rude, is delicate in art.

Morning! The word itself is beautiful,
   And the young hours have many gifts to give
That feed the soul with beauty. He who keeps
His days for labour and his nights for sleep

Wakes conscious of the joy it is to live,
And brings from that mysterious Land of Dreams
A sense of beauty that illumines earth.
Morning! The word itself is beautiful.

The search for beauty is the search for God.

THE INVISIBLE HELPERS

There are, there are
Invisible Great Helpers of the race.
Across unatlased continents of space,
From star to star.
   In answer to some soul's imperious need,
   They speed, they speed.

When the earth-loving young are forced to stand
Upon the border of the Unknown Land,
They come, they come--those angels who have trod
The altitudes of God,
And to the trembling heart
Their strength impart.
   Have you not seen the delicate young maid,
Filled with the joy of life in her fair dawn,
   Look in the face of death, all unafraid,
And smilingly pass on?

This is not human strength; not even faith
   Has such large confidence in such an hour.

It is a power
Supplied by beings who have conquered death.
   Floating from sphere to sphere
   They hover near
The souls that need the courage they can give.

This is no vision of a dreamer's mind.
Though we are blind
They live, they live,
Filling all space -
Invisible Great Helpers of the race.

TO THE WOMEN OF AUSTRALIA

A toast to the splendid daughters
Of the New World over the waters,
   A world that is great as new;
Daughters of brave old races,
Daughters of heights and spaces,
Broad seas and broad earth places -
   Hail to your land and you!

The sun and the winds have fed you;
The width of your world has led you
   Out into the larger view;
Strong with a strength that is tender,
Bright with a primal splendour,
Homage and praise we render -
   Hail to your land and you!

Sisters and daughters and mothers,
Standing abreast with your brothers,
   Working for things that are true;
Thinking and doing and daring,
Giving, receiving, and sharing,
Earning the crowns you are wearing -
   Hail to your land and you!

REPLIES

You have lived long and learned the secret of life, O Seer!
Tell me what are the best three things to seek -
The best three things for a man to seek on earth?

The best three things for a man to seek, O Son! are these:
Reverence for that great Source from whence he came;
Work for the world wherein he finds himself;
And knowledge of the Realm toward which he goes.

What are the best three things to love on earth, O Seer!
What are the best three things for a man to love?

The best three things for a man to love, O Son! are these:
Labour which keeps his forces all in action;
A home wherein no evil thing may enter;
And a loving woman with God in her heart.

What are the three great sins to shun, O Seer! -
What are the three great sins for a man to shun?

The three great sins for a man to shun, O Son! are these:
A thought which soils the heart from whence it goes;
An action that can harm a living thing;
And undeveloped energies of mind.

What are the worst three things to fear, O Seer! -
What are the worst three things for a man to fear?

The worst three things for man to fear, O Son! are these:
Doubt and suspicion in a young child's eyes;
Accusing shame upon a woman's face;
And in himself no consciousness of God.

EARTH BOUND

New paradise, and groom and bride;
The world was all their own;
Her heart swelled full of love and pride;
Yet were they quite alone?
'Now how is it, oh how is it, and why is it' (in fear
All silent to herself she spake) 'that something strange seems here?'

Along the garden paths they walked -
The moon was at its height -
And lover-wise they strolled and talked,
But something was not right.
And 'Who is that, now who is that, oh who is that,' quoth she,
(All silent in her heart she spake) 'that seems to follow me?'

He drew her closer to his side;
She felt his lingering kiss;
And yet a shadow seemed to glide
Between her heart and his.
And 'What is that, now what is that, oh what is that,' she said,
(All silent to herself she spake) 'that minds me of the dead?'

They wandered back by beds of bloom;
They climbed a winding stair;
They crossed the threshold of their room,
But something waited there.
'Now who is this, and what is this, and where is this,' she cried,
(All silent was the cry she made) 'that comes to haunt and hide?'

Wide-eyed she lay, the while he slept;
She could not name her fear.
But something from her bedside crept
Just as the dawn drew near,
(She did not know, she could not know--how could she know?--who came
To haunt the home of one whose hand had dug her grave of shame).

A SUCCESSFUL MAN

There was a man who killed a loving maid
In some mad mood of passion; and he paid
The price, upon a scaffold. Now his name
Stands only as a synonym for shame.
There was another man, who took to wife
A loving woman. She was full of life,
Of hope, and aspirations; and her pride
Clothed her like some rich mantle.

    First, the wide
Glad stream of life that through her veins had sway
He dammed by rocks, cast in it, day by day.
Her flag of hope, flung gaily to the world,
He placed half mast, and then hauled down, and furled.
The aspirations, breathing in each word,
By subtle ridicule, were made absurd:

The delicate fine mantle of her pride,
With rude unfeeling hands, was wrenched aside:
And by mean avarice, or vulgar show,
Her quivering woman's heart was made to know
That she was but a chattel, bought to fill
Whatever niche might please the buyer's will.

So she was murdered, while the slow years went.
And her assassin, honoured, opulent,
Lived with no punishment, or social ban!
'A good provider, a successful man.'

UNSATISFIED

The bird flies home to its young;
The flower folds its leaves about an opening bud;
And in my neighbour's house there is the cry of a child.
I close my window that I need not hear.

She is mine, and she is very beautiful:
And in her heart there is no evil thought.
There is even love in her heart -
Love of life, love of joy, love of this fair world,
And love of me (or love of my love for her);
Yet she will never consent to bear me a child.
And when I speak of it she weeps,
Always she weeps, saying:
'Do I not bring joy enough into your life?
Are you not satisfied with me and my love,
As I am satisfied with you?
Never would I urge you to some great peril
To please my whim; yet ever so you urge me,
Urge me to risk my happiness--yea, life itself -
So lightly do you hold me.' And then she weeps,
Always she weeps, until I kiss away her tears
And soothe her with sweet lies, saying I am content.
Then she goes singing through the house like some bright bird
Preening her wings, making herself all beautiful,
Perching upon my knee, and pecking at my lips
With little kisses. So again love's ship
Goes sailing forth upon a portless sea,
From nowhere unto nowhere; and it takes

Or brings no cargoes to enrich the world.

    The years
Are passing by us. We will yet be old
Who now are young. And all the man in me
Cries for the reproduction of myself
Through her I love. Why, love and youth like ours
Could populate with gods and goddesses
This great, green earth, and give the race new types
Were it made fruitful! Often I can see,
As in a vision, desolate old age
And loneliness descending on us two,
And nowhere in the world, nowhere beyond the earth,
Fruit of my loins and of her womb to feed
Our hungry hearts. To me it seems
More sorrowful than sitting by small graves
And wetting sad-eyed pansies with our tears.

The bird flies home to its young;
The flower folds its leaves about an opening bud;
And in my neighbour's house there is the cry of a child.
I close my window that I need not hear.

S

SEPARATION

HE

One decade and a half since first we came
With hearts aflame
Into Love's Paradise, as man and mate;
And now we separate.
Soon, all too soon,
Waned the white splendour of our honeymoon.
   We saw it fading; but we did not know
    How bleak the path would be when once its glow
Was wholly gone.
And yet we two were forced to follow on -
   Leagues, leagues apart while ever side by side.
    Darker and darker grew the loveless weather,
Darker the way,
Until we could not stay
    Longer together.
  Now that all anger from our hearts has died,
And love has flown far from its ruined nest,
To find sweet shelter in another breast,
   Let us talk calmly of our past mistakes,
   And of our faults; if only for the sakes
Of those with whom our futures will be cast.
   You shall speak first.

SHE

A woman would speak last -

Tell me my first grave error as a wife.

HE

  Inertia. My young veins were rife
With manhood's ardent blood; and love was fire
Within me. But you met my strong desire
   With lips like frozen rose leaves--chaste, so chaste
   That all your splendid beauty seemed but waste
Of love's materials. Then of that beauty
   Which had so pleased my sight
You seemed to take no care; you felt no duty
   To keep yourself an object of delight
   For lover's-eyes; and appetite
And indolence soon wrought
Their devastating changes. You were not
   The woman I had sworn to love and cherish.
If love is starved, what can love do but perish?
Now will you speak of my first fatal sin
   And all that followed, even as I have done?

SHE

I must begin
   With the young quarter of our honeymoon.
  You are but one
   Of countless men who take the priceless boon
Of woman's love and kill it at the start,
   Not wantonly but blindly. Woman's passion
Is such a subtle thing--woof of her heart,
Web of her spirit; and the body's part
  Is to play ever but the lesser role
  To her white soul.

      Seized in brute fashion,
It fades like down on wings of butterflies;
Then dies.
   So my love died.
   Next, on base Mammon's cross you nailed my pride,
   Making me ask for what was mine by right:
   Until, in my own sight,
   I seemed a helpless slave
   To whom the master gave
A grudging dole. Oh, yes, at times gifts showered
Upon your chattel; but I was not dowered
   By generous love. Hate never framed a curse
Or placed a cruel ban
That so crushed woman, as the law of man
   That makes her pensioner upon his purse.
That necessary stuff called gold is such
A cold, rude thing it needs the nicest touch
    Of thought and speech when it approaches love,
    Or it will prove the certain death thereof.

HE

Your words cut deep; 'tis time we separate.

SHE

Well, each goes wiser to a newer mate.

TO THE TEACHERS OF THE YOUNG

How large thy task, O teacher of the young,
To take the ravelled threads by parents flung
With careless hands, and through consummate care
To weave a fabric, fine and firm and fair.
God's uncompleted work is thine to do -
Be brave and true!

BEAUTY MAKING

Methinks there is no greater work in life
Than making beauty. Can the mind conceive
One little corner in celestial realms
Unbeautiful, or dull or commonplace?
Or picture ugly angels, illy clad?
Beauty and splendour, opulence and joy,
Are attributes of God and His domain,
And so are worth and virtue. But why preach
Of virtue only to the sons of men,
Ignoring beauty, till they think it sin?
Why, if each dweller on this little globe
Could know the sacred meaning of that word
And understand its deep significance,
Men's thoughts would form in beauty, till their dreams

Of heaven would find expression in their lives,
However humble; they themselves would grow
Godlike, befitting such a fair estate.
Let us be done with what is only good,
Demanding here and now the beautiful;
Lest, with the mind and eye on earth untrained,
We shall be ill at ease when heaven is gained.

ON AVON'S BREAST I SAW A STATELY SWAN

One day when England's June was at its best,
I saw a stately and imperious swan
Floating on Avon's fair untroubled breast.
Sudden, it seemed as if all strife had gone
Out of the world; all discord, all unrest.

The sorrows and the sinnings of the race
Faded away like nightmares in the dawn.
All heaven was one blue background for the grace
Of Avon's beautiful, slow-moving swan;
And earth held nothing mean or commonplace.

Life seemed no longer to be hurrying on
With unbecoming haste; but softly trod,
As one who reads in emerald leaf, or lawn,
Or crimson rose a message straight from God.
. . . . .
On Avon's breast I saw a stately swan.

THE LITTLE GO-CART

It was long, long ago that a soul like a flower
Unfolded, and blossomed, and passed in an hour.
It was long, long ago; and the memory seems
Like the pleasures and sorrows that come in our dreams.

The kind years have crowned me with many a joy
Since the going away of my wee little boy;
Each one as it passed me has stooped with a kiss,
And left some delight--knowing one thing I miss.

But when in the park or the street, all elate
A baby I see in his carriage of state,
As proud as a king, in his little go-cart -
I feel all the mother-love stir in my heart!

And I seem to be back in that long-vanished May;
And the baby, who came but to hurry away
In the little white hearse, is not dead, but alive,
And out in his little go-cart for a drive.

I whisper a prayer as he rides down the street,
And my thoughts follow after him, tender and sweet;
For I know, by a law that is vast and divine,
(Though I know not his name) that the baby is mine!

I AM RUNNING FORTH TO MEET YOU

I am running forth to meet you, O my Master,
For they tell me you are surely on the way;
Yes, they tell me you are coming back again
(While I run, while I run).
And I wish my feet were winged to speed on faster,
And I wish I might behold you here to-day,
Lord of men.

I am running, yet I walk beside my neighbour,
And I take the duties given me to do;
Yes, I take the daily duties as they fall
(While I run, while I run),
And my heart runs to my hand and helps the labour,
For I think this is the way that leads to you,
Lord of all.

I am running, yet I turn from toil and duty,
Oftentimes to just the art of being glad;
Yes, to just the joys that make the earth-world bright
(While I run, while I run).
For the soul that worships God must worship beauty,
And the heart that thinks of You can not be sad,
Lord of light.

I am running, yet I pause to greet my brother,
And I lean to rid my garden of its weed;
Yes, I lean, although I lift my thoughts above
(While I run, while I run).

And I think of that command, 'Love one another,'
As I hear discordant sounds of creed with creed,
Lord of Love.

I am running, and the road is lit with splendour,
And it brightens and shines fairer with each span;
Yes, it brightens like the highway in a dream
(While I run, while I run).
And my heart to all the world grows very tender,
For I seem to see the Christ in every man,
Lord supreme.

MARTYRS OF PEACE

Fame writes ever its song and story,
For heroes of war, in letters of glory.

But where is the story and where is the song
For the heroes of peace and the martyrs of wrong?

They fight their battles in shop and mine;
They die at their posts and make no sign.

They herd like beasts in a slaughter pen;
They live like cattle and suffer like men.

Why, set by the horrors of such a life,
Like a merry-go-round seems the battle's strife,

And the open sea, and the open boat,
And the deadly cannon with bellowing throat.

Oh, what are they all, with death thrown in,
To the life that has nothing to lose or win -

The life that has nothing to hope or gain
But ill-paid labour and beds of pain?

Fame, where is your story and where is your song
For the martyrs of peace and the victims of wrong?

HOME

The greatest words are always solitaires,
  Set singly in one syllable; like birth,
  Life, love, hope, peace. I sing the worth
Of that dear word toward which the whole world fares -
    I sing of home.

To make a home, we should take all of love
  And much of labour, patience, and keen joy;
  Then mix the elements of earth's alloy
With finer things drawn from the realms above,
    The spirit home.

There should be music, melody and song;
  Beauty in every spot; an open door
    And generous sharing of the pleasure store

With fellow-pilgrims as they pass along,
   Seeking for home.

Make ample room for silent friends--the books,
   That give so much and only ask for space.
   Nor let Utility crowd out the vase
Which has no use save gracing by its looks
   The precious home.

To narrow bounds let mirrors lend their aid
   And multiply each gracious touch of art;
   And let the casual stranger feel the part -
The great creative part--that love has played
   Within the home.

Here bring your best in thought and word and deed,
   Your sweetest acts, your highest self-control;
   Nor save them for some later hour and goal.
Here is the place, and now the time of need,
   Here in your home.

THE ETERNAL NOW

Time with his back against the mighty wall,
   Which hides from view all future joy and sorrow,
Hears, without answer, the impatient call
   Of puny man, to tell him of to-morrow.

Moral, be wise, and to the silence bow,
   These useless and unquiet ways forsaking;
Concern thyself with the Eternal Now -
   To-day hold all things, ready for thy taking.

IF I WERE A MAN, A YOUNG MAN

If I were a man, a young man, and knew what I know to-day,
I would look in the eyes of Life undaunted
   By any Fate that might threaten me.
I would give to the world what the world most wanted -
   Manhood that knows it can do and be;
   Courage that dares, and faith that can see
   Clear into the depths of the human soul,
   And find God there, and the ultimate goal,
If I were a man, a young man, and knew what I know to-day.

If I were a man, a young man, and knew what I know to-day,

I would think of myself as the masterful creature
    Of all the Masterful plan;
The Formless Cause, with form and feature;
    The Power that heeds not limit or ban;
    Man, wonderful man.
I would do good deeds, and forget them straightway;
    I would weave my woes into ropes and climb
Up to the heights of the helper's gateway;
    And Life should serve me, and Time,
    And I would sail out, and out, and find
    The treasures that lie in the deep sea, Mind.
    I would dream, and think, and act;
I would work, and love, and pray,
    Till each dream and vision grew into a fact,
If I were a man, a young man, and knew what I know to-day.

If I were a man, a young man, and knew what I know to-day,
    I would guard my passions as Kings guard treasures,
    And keep them high and clean.
    (For the will of a man, with his passions, measures;
    It is strong as they are keen.)
    I would think of each woman as some one's mother;
    I would think of each man as my own blood brother,
And speed him along on his way.
    And the glory of life in this wonderful hour
    Should fill me and thrill me with Conscious power,
If I were a man, a young man, and knew what I know to-day.

WE MUST SEND THEM OUT TO PLAY

Now much there is need of doing must not be done in haste;
  But slowly and with patience, as a jungle is changed to a town.
    But listen, my brothers, listen; it is not always so:
When a murderer's hand is lifted to kill, there is no time to waste;
  And the way to change his purpose is first to knock him down
    And teach him the law of kindness after you give him the blow.

The acorn you plant in the morning will not give shade at noon;
  And the thornless cactus must be bred by year on year of toil.
    But listen, my brothers, listen; it is not ever the way,
For the roots of the poison ivy plant you cannot pull too soon;
  If you would better your garden and make the most of your soil,
    Hurry and dig up the evil things and cast them out to-day.

The ancient sin of the nations no law can ever efface;
  We must wait for the mothers of men to grow, and give clean souls to their sons.
    But listen, my brothers, listen--when a child cries out in pain,
We must rise from the banquet board and go, though the host is saying grace;
  We must rise and find the Herod of Greed, who is killing our little ones,
    Nor ever go back to the banquet until the monster is slain.

The strong man waits for justice, with lifted soul and eyes,
  As a sturdy oak will face the storm, and does not break or bow.
    But listen, my brothers, listen; the child is a child for a

day;
If a merciless foot treads down each shoot, how can the forest rise?
   We are robbing the race when we rob a child; we must rescue the children NOW;
     We must rescue the little slaves of Greed and send them out to play.

PROTEST

To sit in silence when we should protest
Makes cowards out of men. The human race
Has climbed on protest. Had no voice been raised
Against injustice, ignorance and lust
The Inquisition yet would serve the law
And guillotines decide our least disputes.
The few who dare must speak and speak again
To right the wrongs of many. Speech, thank God,
No vested power in this great day and land
Can gag or throttle; Press and voice may cry
Loud disapproval of existing ills,
May criticise oppression and condemn
The lawlessness of wealth-protecting laws
That let the children and child-bearers toil
To purchase ease for idle millionaires,
Therefore do I protest against the boast
Of independence in this mighty land.
Call no chain strong which holds one rusted link,
Call no land free that holds one fettered slave
Until the manacled, slim wrists of babes

Are loosed to toss in childish sport and glee,
Until the Mother bears no burden save
The precious one beneath her heart; until
God's soil is rescued from the clutch of greed
And given back to labour, let no man
Call this the Land of Freedom.

REWARD

Fate used me meanly; but I looked at her and laughed,
That none might know how bitter was the cup I quaffed.
Along came Joy, and paused beside me where I sat,
Saying, 'I came to see what you were laughing at.'

THIS IS MY TASK

When the whole world resounds with rude alarms
Of warring arms,
When God's good earth, from border unto border
Shows man's disorder,
Let me not waste my dower of mortal might
In grieving over wrongs I cannot right.
This is my task: amid discordant strife
To keep a clean sweet centre in my life;

And though the human orchestra may be
Playing all out of key -
To tune my soul to symphonies above,
And sound the note of love.
This is my task.

When by the minds of men most beauteous Faith
Seems doomed to death,
And to her place is hoisted, by soul treason,
The dullard Reason,
Let me not hurry forth with flag unfurled
To proselyte an unbelieving world.
This is my task: in depths of unstarred night
Or in diverting and distracting light
To keep (in crowds, or in my room alone)
Faith on her lofty throne;
And whatsoever happen or befall,
To see God's hand in all.
This is my task.

When, in church pews, men worship God in words,
But meet their kind with swords,
When Fair Religion, stripped of holy passion,
Walks masked as Fashion,
Let me not wax indignant at the sight;
Or waste my strength bewailing her sad plight.
This is my task: to search in my own mind
Until the qualities of God I find;
To seek them in the hearts of friend and foe -
Or high or low;
And in my hours of toil, or prayer, or play,
To live my creed each day.
This is my task.

THE STATUE

A granite rock in the mountain side
Gazed on the world and was satisfied.
It watched the centuries come and go,
It welcomed the sunlight yet loved the snow,
It grieved when the forest was forced to fall,
Yet joyed when steeples rose white and tall
In the valley below it, and thrilled to hear
The voice of the great town roaring near.

When the mountain stream from its idle play
Was caught by the mill-wheel and borne away
And trained to labour, the gray rock mused,
'Tree and verdure and stream are used
By man the master, but I remain
Friend of the mountain and star and plain,
Unchanged forever by God's decree
While passing centuries bow to me.'

Then all unwarned, with a mighty shock
Out of the mountain was wrenched the rock;
Bruised and battered, and broken in heart
It was carried away to the common mart.
Wrenched, and ruined in peace and pride,
'Oh, God is cruel,' the granite cried,
'Comrade of mountain, of star the friend,
By all deserted--how sad my end.'

A dreaming sculptor in passing by

Gazed on the granite with thoughtful eye;
Then stirred with a purpose supremely grand
He bade his dream in the rock expand.
And lo! from the broken and shapeless mass
That grieved and doubted, it came to pass
That a glorious statue of priceless worth
And infinite beauty adorned the earth.

BEHOLD THE EARTH

Behold the earth swung in among the stars
Fit home for gods if men were only kind -
Do thou thy part to shape it to those ends,
By shaping thine own life to perfectness.
Seek nothing for thyself or thine own kin
That robs another of one hope or joy,
Let no man toil in poverty and pain
To give thee unearned luxury and ease.
Feed not the hungry servitor with stones,
That idle guests may fatten on thy bread.
Look for the good in stranger and in foe,
Nor save thy praises for the cherished few;
And let the weakest sinner find in thee
An impetus to reach receding heights.
Behold the earth swung in among the stars -
Fit home for gods; wake thou the God within
And by the broad example of thy love
Communicate Omnipotence to men.
All men are unawakened gods: be thine
The voice to rouse them from unhappy sleep

WHAT THEY SAW

Sad man, Sad man, tell me, pray,
What did you see to-day?

I saw the unloved and unhappy old, waiting for slow delinquent death to come.
Pale little children toiling for the rich, in rooms where sunlight is ashamed to go.
The awful alms-house, where the living dead rot slowly in their hideous open graves.
And there were shameful things;
Soldiers and forts, and industries of death, and devil ships, and loud-winged devil birds,
All bent on slaughter and destruction. These and yet more shameful things mine eyes beheld.
Old men upon lascivious conquest bent, and young men living with no thought of God;
And half clothed women puffing at a weed, aping the vices of the underworld -
Engrossed in shallow pleasures and intent on being barren wives.
These things I saw.
(How God must loathe His earth.)

Glad man, Glad man, tell me, pray,
What did you see to-day?

I saw an aged couple, in whose eyes
Shone that deep light of mingled love and faith
Which makes the earth one room of Paradise,

And leaves no sting in death.

I saw fair regiments of children pour,
Rank after rank, out of the schoolroom door
By Progress mobilised. They seemed to say
'Let ignorance make way;
We are the heralds of a better day.'

I saw the college and the church that stood
For all things sane and good.

I saw God's helpers in the shop and slum
Blazing a path for health and hope to come;
And men and women of large soul and mind
Absorbed in toil for bettering their kind.

Then, too, I saw life's sweetest sight and best -
Pure mothers with dear babies at the breast,
These things I saw.
(How God must love His earth.)

HIS LAST LETTER

Well, you are free;
The longed for, lied for, waited for decree
Is yours to-day.
I made no protest; and you had your say,
And left me with no vestige of repute.
Neglect, abuse, and cruelty you charge
With broken marriage vows. The list is large
But not to be denied. So I was mute.

Now you shall listen to a few plain facts
Before you go out wholly from my life
As some man's wife.
Read carefully this statement of your acts
Which changed the lustre of my honeymoon
To sombre gloom,
And wrenched the cover from Pandora's box.

In those first talks
'Twixt bride and groom I showed you my whole heart,
Showed you how deep my love was and how true;
With all a strong man's feeling I loved YOU:
(God, how I loved you, my one chosen mate.)
But I learned this
(So poorly did you play your little part):
You married marriage, to avoid the fate
Of having 'Miss'
Carved on your tombstone. Love you did not know,
But you were greedy for the showy things

That money brings.
Such weak affection as you could bestow
Was given the provider, not the lover.

The knowledge hurt. Keen pain like that is dumb;
And masks itself in smiles, lest men discover.
But I was lonely; and the feeling grew
The more I studied you.
Into your shallow heart love could not come,
But yet you loved my love; because it gave
The prowess of a mistress o'er a slave.
You showed your power
In petty tyranny hour after hour,
Day after day, year after lengthening years.
My tasks, my pleasures, my pursuits were not
Held near or dear,
Or made to seem important in your thought.
My friends were not your friends; you goaded me
By foolish and ignoble jealousy,
Till, through suggestion's laws
I gave you cause.
The beauteous ideal Love had hung
In my soul's shrine,
And worshipped as a something all divine,
With wanton hand you flung
Into the dust. And then you wondered why
My love should die.
My sins and derelictions cry aloud
To all the world: my head is bowed
Under its merited reproaches. Yours
Is lifted to receive
The sympathy the court's decree insures.
The world loves to believe

In man's depravity and woman's worth;
But I am one of many men on earth
Whose loud resounding fall
Is like the crashing of some well-built wall
Which those who seek can trace
To the slow work of insects at its base.
. . . .
Be not afraid.
The alimony will be promptly paid

A DIALOGUE

HE

Let us be friends. My life is sad and lonely,
While yours with love is beautiful and bright.
Be kind to me: I ask your friendship only.
No Star is robbed by lending darkness light.

SHE

I give you friendship as I understand it,
A sentiment I feel for all mankind.

HE

Oh, give me more; may not one friend command it?

SHE

Look in the skies, 'tis there the star you'll find;
It casts its beams on all with equal favour.

HE

I would have more than what all men may claim.

SHE

Then your ideas of friendship strongly savour
Of sentiments which wear another name.

HE

May not one friend receive more than another?

SHE

Not man from woman and still remain a friend.
Life holds but three for her, a father, brother,
Lover--against the rest she must contend.

HE

Against the universe I would protect you,
With my life even, nor hold the price too dear.

SHE

But not against YOURSELF, should fate select you
As Lancelot for foolish Guinevere.

HE

You would not tempt me?

SHE

That is undisputed.
We put the question back upon the shelf.
My point remains unanswered, unrefuted
No man protects a woman from himself.

HE

I am immune: for once I loved with passion,
And all the fires within me burned to dust.
I think of woman but in friendly fashion:
In me she finds a comrade safe to trust.

SHE

So said Mount Peelee to the listening ocean:
Behold what followed! Let the good be wise.
Though human hearts proclaim extinct emotion,
Beware how high the tides of friendship rise.

A WISH

Great dignity ever attends great grief,
And silently walks beside it;
And I always know when I see such woe
That Invisible Helpers guide it.
And I know deep sorrow is like a tide,
It cannot ever be flowing;
The high-water mark in the night and the dark -
Then dawn, and the outward going.

But the people who pull at my heart-strings hard
Are the ones whom destiny hurries
Through commonplace ways to the end of their days,
And pesters with paltry worries.
The peddlers who trudge with a budget of wares
To the door that is slammed unkindly;
The vendor who stands with his shop in his hands
Where the hastening hosts pass blindly;

The woman who holds in her poor flat purse
The price of her rent-room only,
While her starved eye feeds on the comfort she needs
To brighten the lot that is lonely;
The man in the desert of endless work,
Unsoftened by islands of leisure;
And the children who toil in the dust and the soil,
While their little hearts cry for pleasure;

The people who labour, and scrimp, and save,
At the call of some thankless duty,
And carefully hide, with a mien of pride,
Their ravening hunger for beauty;
These ask no pity, and seek no aid,
But the thought of them somehow is haunting;
And I wish I might fling at their feet everything
That I know in their hearts they are wanting.

JUSTICE

However inexplicable may seem
Event and circumstance upon the earth,
Though favours fall on those who none esteem,
And insult and indifference greet worth,
Though poverty repays a life of toil,
And riches spring where idle feet have trod,
And storms lay waste the patiently tilled soil -
Yet Justice sways the universe of God.

As undisturbed the stately stars remain
Beyond the glare of day's obscuring light,
So Justice dwells, though mortal eyes in vain
Seek it persistently by reason's sight.
But, when once freed, the illumined soul looks out -
Its cry will be, 'O God, how could I doubt?'

AN OLD SONG

Two roadways lead from this land to That, and one is the road of Prayer;
And one is the road of Old-time Songs, and every note is a stair.

A shabby old man with a music machine on the sordid city street;
But suddenly earth seemed Arcady, and life grew young and sweet.
For the city street fled, and the world was green, and a little house stood by the sea;
And she came singing a martial air (she who was peace itself);
She brought back with her the old, strange charm, of mingled pathos and glee -

With her eyes of a child in a woman's face, and her soul of a saint in an elf.
She had been gone for many a year. They tell us it is not far -
That silent place where the dear ones go, but it might as well be a star.
Yes, it might as well be a distant star as a beautiful Near-by Land,
If we hear no voice, and see no face, and feel no touch of a hand.

But now she had come, for I saw her there, and she looked so blithe and young;
(Not white and still, as I saw her last) and the rose that she wore was red;
And her voice soared up in a bird-like trill, at the end of the song she sung,
And she mimicked a soldier's warlike stride, and tossed back her dear little head.

She had gone for many a year, and never came back before;
But I think she dwells in a Near-by Land, since song jarred open the door;
Yes, I think it is surely a Near-by Land, that place where our loved ones are,
For the song would never have reached her ear had she been on a distant star.

Two roadways lead from this land to That, and one is the road of Prayer,
And one is the road of Old-time Songs, and every note is a stair.

OH, POOR, SICK WORLD

Lord of all the Universe, when I think of YOU,
Flinging stars out into space, moving suns and tides;
Then this little mortal mind gets the larger view,
And the carping self of me runs away and hides.

Then I see all shadowed paths leading out to Light;
See the false things fade away, leaving but the True;
See the wrong things slay themselves, leaving only Right;
When this little mortal mind gets the larger view.

Cavillings at this and that, censure, doubt and fear,
Fly, as fly before the dawn, insects of the night;
Life and Death are understood; everything seems clear,
All the wrong things slay themselves, leaving only Right.

The World has walked with fever in its veins
For many and many a day. Oh, poor, sick world!
Not knowing all its dreams of greed and gain,
Of selfish conquest and possession, were
Disordered visions of a brain diseased.

Now the World's malady is at its height
And there is foul contagion in its breath.
It raves of death and slaughter; and the stars
Shake with reverberations of its cries,
And the sad seas are troubled and disturbed.
So must it rave--this sick and suffering world -
Until the old secretions in its blood
Are emptied out and purged away by war;
And the deep seated cankers of the mind
Begin the healing process. Then a calm
Shall come upon the earth; and that loved word
PEACE, shall be understood from shore to shore.

Shriek on, mad world. The great Physician sits
Serenely conscious of the coming change,
Nor seeks to check the fever; it must run
Until its course is finished. He can wait.

In his vast Solar Systems he has seen
So many other worlds as sick as this
He feels but pity for his ailing charge,
Not blame or anger. And he knows the hour
Will surely dawn when that sick child shall wake
Free from all frenzied fancies, and shall turn
Clear-seeing eyes upon the face of God.
Then shall begin the new millennium.

Lord of all the Universe, when I think of YOU,
Then this little mortal mind gets the larger view;
Then I see all shadowed paths leading into Light,
Where the wrong things slay themselves, leaving only Right.

Oh, poor, sick world!

PRAISE DAY

Let us halt now for a space in our hurrying;
Let us take time to look up and look out;
Let us refuse for a spell to be worrying;
Let us decline to both question and doubt.
If one goes cavilling,
Hair splitting, flaw hunting--ready for strife -
All the best pleasure is missed in the travelling
Onward through life.

Just for to-day we will put away sorrowing -
Just for to-day not a tear shall be shed;
Nor will we fear anything, or go borrowing
Pain from the future by profitless dread.
Thought shall go frolicking,
Pleasuring, treasuring everything bright -
Tasting the joy that is found just in rollicking
On through the light.

Just for to-day all the ills that need bettering
We will omit from our notebook of mind;

All that is good we will mark by red-lettering; -
Those things alone we are seeking to find.
Things to be sad over,
Pine over, whine over--pass them, I say!
Nothing is noted save what we are glad over -
This is Praise Day.

INTERLUDE

The days grow shorter, the nights grow longer;
The headstones thicken along the way;
And life grows sadder, but love grows stronger,
For those who walk with us day by day.

The tear comes quicker, the laugh comes slower;
The courage is lesser to do and dare;
And the tide of joy in the heart falls lower,
And seldom covers the reefs of care.

But all true things in the world seem truer;
And the better things of earth seem best;
And friends are dearer, as friends are fewer,
And love is all, as our sun dips west.

Then let us clasp hands as we walk together,
And let us speak softly in love's sweet tone;
For no man knows on the morrow whether
We two pass on--or but one alone.

THE LAND OF THE GONE-AWAY-SOULS

Oh! that is a beautiful land I wis,
The land of the Gone-Away Souls.
Yes, a lovelier region by far than this
(Though this is a world most fair),
The goodliest goal of all good goals,
Else why do our friends stay there?
I walk in a world that is sweet with friends,
And earth I have ever held dear;
Yes, love with duty and beauty blends,
To render the earth plane bright.
But faster and faster, year on year
My comrades hurry from sight.

They hurry away to the Over-There,
And few of them say Farewell.
Yes, they go away with a secret air
As if on a secret quest.
And they come not back to the earth to tell
Why that land seems the best.

Messages come from the mystic sphere,
But few know the code of that land;
Yes, many the message, but few who hear
In the din of the world below,
Or hearing the message, can understand
Those truths which we long to know.

But it must be the goal of all good goals,

And I think of it more and more,
Yes I think of that land of the Gone-Away-Souls
And its growing host of friends
Who will hail my bark when it touches shore
Where the last brief journey ends.

THE HARP'S SONG

All day, all day in a calm like death
The harp hung waiting the sea wind's breath.

When the western sky flushed red with shame
At the sun's bold kiss, the sea wind came.

Said the harp to the breeze, Oh, breathe as soft
As the ring-dove cooes from its nest aloft.

I am full of a song that mothers croon
When their wee ones tire of their play at noon.

Though a harp may feel 'tis a silent thing
Till the breeze arises and bids it sing.

Said the wind to the harp, Nay, sing for me
The wail of the dead that are lost at sea.

I caught their cry as I came along,
And I hurried to find you and teach you the song.

Oh, the heart is the harp, and love is the breeze,
And the song is ever what love may please.

THE PENDULUM

[In Edgar Allan Poe's story, 'The Pit and the Pendulum,' the victim is bound hand and foot, face upturned to a huge, knife-edged pendulum which swings back and forth across his body, the blade dropping closer to his heart at each swing.]

Bound hand and foot in the pit I lie,
And the wall about me is strong and high;
Stronger and higher it grows each day,
With maximum labour and minimum pay;
And there is no ladder whereon to climb
To a fairer world and a brighter time.
There is no ladder, there is no rope,
But the devil of greed has given a hope.
He swings before me the pendulum--Vice;
I know its purpose and know its price,
And the world's good people all know it, too,
And much they chatter and little they do.
I have sent up my cry to the hosts of men
Over and over and over again:
But should I cry once to the devil, ah, he
Would hurry to answer and set me free.
For Virtue to Virtue must ever call thrice,
But once brings an answer when Virtue calls Vice.

Bound hand and foot in the pit I lie
While the pendulum swings and the days go by.

AN OLD-FASHIONED TYPE

For 'Mabel Brown' I never cared
  (My rightful name by birth),
But when the name of Smith I shared,
  I seemed to own the earth,
(I wrote it without 'y' or 'e' -
Plain 'Mrs. Jack Smith' suited me.)

My happiest hour, as I look back
  On times of great content,
Was when folks called me 'Mrs. Jack,'
  Though 'Mrs. Smith' was meant.
It was the pleasure of my life
To hear them say: 'That's Jack Smith's wife.'

One day I joined a club. They said
  That I must speak or write.
So I did both. I wrote and read
  A speech one fateful night.
It made a hit, but proved, alack,
A death blow to poor 'Mrs. Jack.'

As 'Mrs. Mabel Smith' I'm known
  Throughout my town and State;
My heart feels widowed and alone;

The case is intricate.
Though darling Jack is mine, the same,
I am divorced somehow in name.

Just 'Mabel Smith' I can endure;
  It leaves the world in doubt;
But 'Mrs.' makes the marriage sure,
  Yet leaves the husband out.
It sounds like Reno, or the tomb,
And always fills me full of gloom.

They say the honours are all mine;
  Well, I would trade the pack
For one sweet year in which to shine
  Again as 'Mrs. Jack.'
That gave to life a core, a pith,
Not found by 'Mrs. Mabel Smith.'

For one suggests the chosen mate,
  And all the joy love brings;
And one suggests a delegate
  To federated things.
I'm built upon the old-time plan -
I like to supplement a man.

If on each point of glory's star
  My name shone like a pearl,
I'd feel a pleasure greater far
  In being 'Jack Smith's girl.'
It is ridiculous, I know,
But then, you see, I'm fashioned so.

THE SWORD

Amidst applauding cheers I won a prize.
A cynic watched me, with ironic eyes;
An open foe, in open hatred, sneered;
I cared for neither. Then my friend appeared.
Eager, I listened for his glad 'Well done.'
But sudden shadow seemed to shroud my sun.
He praised me: yet each slow, unwilling word
Forced from its sheath base Envy's hidden sword,
Two-edged, it wounded me; but, worst of all,
It thrust my friend down from his pedestal,
And showed him as he was--so small, so small.

LOVE AND THE SEASONS

SPRING

A sudden softness in the wind;
   A glint of song, a-wing;
A fragrant sound that trails behind,
   And joy in everything.

A sudden flush upon the cheek,
   The teardrop quick to start;
A hope too delicate to speak,
   And heaven within the heart.

SUMMER

A riotous dawn and the sea's great wonder;
   The red, red heart of a rose uncurled;
And beauty tearing her veil asunder,
   In sight of a swooning world.

A call of the soul, and the senses blended;
   The Springtime lost in the glow of the sun,
And two lives rushing, as God intended,
   To meet and mingle as one.

AUTUMN

The world is out in gala dress;
   And yet it is not gay.

Its splendour hides a loneliness
   For something gone away.

(Laughter and music on the air;
   A shower of rice and bloom.
Smiles for the fond departing pair -
   And then the empty room.)

WINTER

Two trees swayed in the winter wind; and dreamed
The snowflakes falling about them were bees
Singing among the leaves. And they were glad,
Knowing the dream would soon come true.

Beside the hearth an aged couple rocked,
And dozed; and dreamed the friends long passed from sight
Were with them once again. They woke and smiled,
Knowing the dream would soon come true.

A NAUGHTY LITTLE COMET

There was once a little comet who lived near the Milky Way!
She loved to wander out at night and jump about and play.
The mother of the comet was a very good old star -
She used to scold her reckless child for venturing out too far;
She told her of the ogre, Sun, who loved on stars to sup,
And who asked no better pastimes than gobbling comets up.

But instead of growing cautious and of showing proper fear,
The foolish little comet edged up near, and near, and near.
She switched her saucy tail along right where the Sun could see,
And flirted with old Mars and was bold as bold could be.
She laughed to scorn the quiet stars, who never frisked about;
She said there was no fun in life unless you ventured out.

She liked to make the planets stare, and wished no better mirth
Than just to see the telescopes aimed at her from the Earth.
She wondered how so many stars could mope through nights and days,
And let the sickly faced old moon get all the love and praise.
And as she talked and tossed her head and switched her shining trail,
The staid old mother star grew sad, her cheek grew wan and pale.

For she had lived there in the skies a million years or more,
And she had heard gay comets talk in just this way before.
And by and by there came an end to this gay comet's fun -
She went a tiny bit too far--and vanished in the Sun!
No more she swings her shining trail before the whole world's sight,
But quiet stars she laughed to scorn are twinkling every night.

THE LAST DANCE

WHEN LOVE FOR HIS MAKER AWOKE IN MAN, THE DANCE BEGAN

The wave of the ocean, the leaf of the wood,
In the rhythm of motion proclaim life is good.
The stars are all swinging to metres and rhyme,
The planets are singing while suns mark the time.
The moonbeams and rivers float off in a trance,
The Universe quivers--on, on with the dance!

Our partners we pick from the best of the throng
In the ballroom of Life and go lilting along;
We follow our fancy, and choose as we will,
For waltz or for tango or merry quadrille;
But ever one partner is waiting us all
At the end of the programme, to finish the ball.

Unasked, and unwelcome, he comes without leave
And calls when he chooses, 'My dance, I believe?'
And none may refuse him, and none may say no;
When he beckons the dancer, the dancer must go.
You may hate him, and shun him; and yet in life's ball
For the one who lives well 'tis the best dance of all.

A VAGABOND MIND

Since early this morning the world has seemed surging
   With unworded rhythm, and rhyme without thought.
It may be the Muses take this way of urging
   The patience and pains by which poems are wrought.
It may be some singer who passed into glory,
   With songs all unfinished, is lingering near
And trying to tell me the rest of the story,
   Which I am too dull of perception to hear.

I hear not, I see not; but feel the sweet swinging
   And swaying of metre, in sunlight and shade,
The still arch of Space with such music is ringing
   As never an audible orchestra made.
The moments glide by me, and each one is dancing;
   Aquiver with life is each leaf on the tree,
And out on the ocean is movement entrancing,
   As billow with billow goes racing with glee.

With never a thought that is worthy the saying,
   And never a theme to be put into song,
Since early this morning my mind has been straying,
   A vagabond thing, with a vagabond throng,
With gay, idle moments, and waves of the ocean,
   With winds and with sunbeams, and tree-tops and birds,
It has lilted along in the joy of mere motion,
   To songs without music and verse without words.

MY FLOWER ROOM

My Flower Room is such a little place,
Scarce twenty feet by nine; yet in that space
I have met God; yea, many a radiant hour
Have talked with Him, the All-Embracing-Cause,
About His laws.
And He has shown me, in each vine and flower
Such miracles of power
That day by day this Flower Room of mine
Has come to be a shrine.

Fed by the self-same soil and atmosphere
Pale, tender shoots appear
Rising to greet the light in that sweet room.
One speeds to crimson bloom;
One slowly creeps to unassuming grace;
One climbs, one trails;
One drinks the light and moisture;
One exhales.

Up through the earth together, stem by stem
Two plants push swiftly in a floral race;
Till one sends forth a blossom like a gem;
And one gives only fragrance
In a seed
So small it scarce is felt within the hand.
Lie hidden such delights
Of scents and sights,
When by the elements of Nature freed,

As Paradise must have at its command.

From shapeless roots and ugly bulbous things
What gorgeous beauty springs!
Such infinite variety appears
A hundred artists in a hundred years
Could never copy from the floral world
The marvels that in leaf and bud lie curled.
Nor could the most colossal mind of man
Create one little seed of plant or vine
Without assistance from the First Great Plan;
Without the aid divine.

Who but a God
Could draw from light and moisture, heat and cold,
And fashion in earth's mould,
A multitude of blooms to deck one sod?
Who but a God!
Not one man knows
Just why the bloom and fragrance of the rose
Or how its tints were blent;
Or why the white Camelia without scent
Up through the same soil grows;
Or how the daisy and the violet
And blades of grass first on wild meadows met.
Not one, not one man knows;
The wisest but SUPPOSE.

This Flower Room of mine
Has come to be a shrine;
And I go hence
Each day with larger faith and reverence.

MY FAITH

My faith is rooted in no written creed;
And there are those who call me heretic;
Yet year on year, though I be well or sick
Or opulent, or in the slough of need,
If, light of foot, fair Life trips by me pleasuring,
Or, by the rule of pain, old Time stands measuring
The dull, drab moments--still ascends my cry:
'God reigns on high!
He doeth all things well!'

Not much I prize, or one, or any brand
Of theologic lore; nor think too well
Of generally accepted heaven and hell.
But faith and knowledge build at Love's command
A beauteous heaven; a heaven of thought all clarified
Of hate and fear and doubt; a heaven of rarefied
And perfect trust; and from the heaven I cry:
'God reigns on high!
Whatever is, is best.'

My faith refuses to accept the 'fall'!
It sees man ever as a child of God,
Growing in wisdom as new realms are trod,
Until the Christ in him is One with All.
From this full consciousness my faith is borrowing
Light to illuminate Life's darkest sorrowing,
Whatever woes assail me still I cry:
'God reigns on high!

He doeth all things well.'

My faith finds prayer the language of the heart,
Which gives us converse with the host unseen;
And those who linger in the vales between
The Here and Yonder, in these prayers take part.
My dead come near, and say: 'Death means not perishing;
Cherish us in your thoughts, for by that cherishing
Shall severed links be welded by and by.'
'God reigns on high!
Whatever is, is best.'

ARROW AND BOW

It is easy to stand in the pulpit, or in the closet to kneel,
    And say: 'God do this; God do that! -
Make the world better; relieve the sorrows of man; for the sake of
Thy Son,
Oh, forgive all sin!' Then, having planned out God's work, to feel
    Our duty is done.
It is easy to be religious this way -
Easy to pray.

It is harder to stand on the highway, or walk in the crowded mart;
    And say: 'I am He. I am He.
'Mine the world-burden; mine the sorrows of men; mine the Christ-work
'To forgive my brother's sin,' and then to live the Christ-part and
never to shirk.
    It is hard for you and me

To be religious this way,
Day after day.

But God is no longer in heaven; we drove Him out with our prayers,
Drove Him out with our sermons and creeds, and our endless plaints and despairs.
He came down over the borders, and Christ, too, came along;
They are looking the whole world over to see just what is wrong.
God has grown weary of hearing His praises sung on earth;
And Jesus is weary of hearing the story about His birth;
And the way to win Their favour, that is surer than any other,
Is to join in a song of Brotherhood and praises of one another.

No; God is no longer in heaven; He has come down on earth to see
That nothing is wrong with the world He made; THE WRONG IS IN YOU AND
ME.
He meant the earth for a garden-spot, where mill and factory stand;
Childhood, he meant for growing-time--but look at the toiling band!
Woman was meant for mother and mate--now look at the slaves of lust.
And the good folks shake their heads and say, 'We must pray to God and trust.'
God has a billion books of our prayers unopened upon his shelves,
For the things we are begging Him to do, He wants us to do ourselves.

Jehovah, Jesus, and each soul in space
  Are one and undividable. Until
We see God shining in each neighbour's face
And find Him in ourselves and hail Him there,
What use is prayer?
  Let us be still.
How can we love the whole and not each part?
How worship God, and harbour in the heart

Hate of God's members--for all men are that.
Too long our souls have sat,
Like poor blind beggars at the door of God.
   He never made a beggar--we are kings!

Let us rise up, for it is time we trod
   The mountain-tops; time that we did the things
We have so long asked God to do.
He waits for you
To look deep in your brother's eyes and see
   The God within;
To hear you say 'Lo, thou art He; Lo, thou art He.'
This is the only way to end all sin,
The difficult, one way.

A prayer without a deed is an arrow without a bow-string;
A deed without a prayer is a bow-string without an arrow.
The heart of a man should be like a quiver full of arrows,
And the hand of a man should be like a strong bow strung for action.
The heart of a man should keep his arrows ever ascending,
And the hand and the mind of a man should keep at a work unending.

IF WE SHOULD MEET HIM

Now what were the words of Jesus,
And what would He pause and say,
If we were to meet in home or street
The Lord of the world to-day?
Oh, I think He would pause and say,
'Go on with your chosen labour;
Speak only good of your neighbour;
Widen your farms, and lay down your arms,
Or dig up the soil with each sabre.'

Now what were the answer of Jesus
If we should ask for a creed
To carry us straight through the wonderful gate
When soul from body is freed?
Oh, I think He would give us this creed:
'Praise God, whatever betide you;
Cast joy on the lives beside you;
Better the earth, by growing in worth,
With love as the law to guide you.'

Now what were the answer of Jesus
If we should ask Him to tell
Of the last great goal of the homing soul,
Where each of us hopes to dwell.
Oh, I think it is this He would tell:
'The soul is the builder--then wake it;
The mind is the kingdom--then take it;
And thought upon thought let Eden be wrought,
For heaven will be what you make it.'

FAITH

Let a valiant Faith cross swords with Death,
And Death is certain to fall;
For the dead arise with joy in their eyes -
They were not dead at all.
If this were only a world of chance,
Then faith, with its strong white spark
Could burn through the sod and fashion a God,
And set Him to shine in the dark.

So in troublesome days, and in shadowy ways,
In the dire and difficult time,
We must cling, we must cling to our Faith, and bring
Our courage to heights sublime.
It is not a matter of hugging a creed
That will lift us up to the light,
But in keeping our trust that Love is just,
And that whatever is, is right.

When the hopes of this world into chaos are hurled,
And the devil seems running the earth,
When the bad folks stay and the good pass away,
And greed fares better than worth,
Oh, that is the hour to trust in the Power
That will straighten the tangle out;
For death and sorrow are little things,
But a terrible thing is doubt.

THE SECRET OF PRAYER

For he who climbs to say his prayer
Meets half way the descending Grace.

ELSA BARKER, in British Review.

This is the secret of all prayers
   That in God's sight have worth,
They must be uttered from the stairs
   That wind away from earth;
And he who mounts to speak the word,
He shall be heard. He shall be heard.

And he who will not leave himself,
   But stays down with his cares,
Or with his thoughts of pride and pelf,
   Though loud and long his prayers,
Beyond earth's dome of arching skies
They shall not rise   They shall not rise.

Oh, ye who seek for strength and power
   Seek first some quiet spot,
And fashion through a silent hour
   Your stairway, thought by thought;
Then climb, and pray to God on high:
He shall reply. He shall reply.

THE ANSWER

Up to the gates of gleaming Pearl,
There came the spirit of a girl,
And to the white-robed Guard she said:
'Dear Angel, am I truly dead?
Just yonder, lying on my bed,
I heard them say it; and they wept.
And after that, methinks I slept.
Then when I woke, I saw your face,
And suddenly was in this place.
It seems a pleasant place to be,
Yet earth was fair enough to me.
What is there here, to do, or see?
Will I see God, dear Angel, say?
And is He very far away?'

The Angel said, 'You are in truth
What men call dead. That word to youth
Is full of terror; but it means
Only a change of tasks, and scenes.
You have been brought to us because
Of certain ancient karmic laws
Set into motion aeons gone.
By us you will be guided on
From plane to plane, and sphere to sphere,
Until your tasks are finished here.
Then back to earth, the home of man,
To work again another span.'

'But, Angel, when will I see God?'

'After the final path is trod;
After you no more long, or crave,
To see, or hear, or own, or have
Aught beside--HIM. Then shall His face
Reveal itself to you in space.
And you shall find yourself made one
With that Great Sun, behind the sun.
Child, go thy way inside the gate,
Where many eager loved ones wait.
Death is but larger life begun.'

A VISION

My soul beheld a vision of the Master:
   Methought He stood with grieved and questioning eyes,
Where Freedom drove its chariot to disaster
   And toilers heard, unheeding, toilers' cries.
Where man withheld God's bounties from his neighbour,
   And fertile fields were sterilised by greed;
Where Labour's hand was lifted against labour,
   And suffering serfs to despots turned when freed.

Majestic rose tall steeple after steeple;
   Imperious bells called worshippers to prayer;
But as they passed, the faces of the people
   Were marred by envy, anger and despair.
'Christ the Redeemer of the world has risen,

Peace and good will,' so rang the major strain;
But forth from sweat-shops, tenement and prison
　　Wailed minor protests, redolent with pain.

Methought about the Master, all unseeing,
　　Fought desperate hosts of striking clan with clan,
Their primal purpose, meant for labour's freeing,
　　Sunk in vindictive hate of man for man.
Pretentious Wealth, in unearned robes of beauty,
　　Flung Want a pittance from her bulging purse,
While ill-paid Toil went on dull rounds of duty,
　　Hell in her heart, and on her lips a curse.

Then spoke the Christ (so wondrous was my vision)
　　(Deep, deep, His voice, with sorrow's cadence fraught):
'This world to-day would be a realm elysian
　　Had my disciples lived the love I taught.
Un-Christlike is the Christian creed men fashion
　　Who kneel to worship, and who rise to slay.
Profane pretenders of my holy Passion,
　　Ye nail Me newly to the cross each day.'

THE SECOND COMING

How will Christ come back again,
How will He be seen, and where,
   Where His chosen way?
Will He come in dead of night,
Shining in His robes of light,
   Or at dawn of day?

Will it be at Christmas time,
When the bells are all achime,
   That He is re-born?
Or will He return and bring
Wide and wondrous wakening
   On some Easter morn?

When will this sad world rejoice,
Listening to that golden voice
   Speaking unto men?
Lives there one who yet shall cry
Loud to startled passers-by -
   'Christ has come again?'

List the answer--Christ is here!
Seek and you shall find him near -
   Dwelling on the earth.
By the world's awakened thought,
This great miracle is wrought,
   This the second birth.

While you wonder where and now
Christ shall come--behold him NOW,
   Patient, loving, meek.
Looking from your neighbour's eyes,
Or in humble toiling guise -
   Lo! the Christ you seek.

Look for him in human hearts,
In the shops, and in the marts,
   And beside your hearth.
Search and speak the watchword Love,
And the Christ shall rise and prove
   He has come to earth.

Sorrowful ofttimes is He
That we have not eyes to see,
   Have not ears to hear,
As we call to Him afar,
Out beyond some distant star,
   While He stands so near.

Seek Him, seek Him, where He dwells,
Chime the voices of the bells
   On the Christmas air.
Christ has come to earth again,
He is in the hearts of men,
   Seek and find him there.

www.bookjungle.com *email: sales@bookjungle.com fax: 630-214-0564 mail: Book Jungle PO Box 2226 Champaign, IL 61825*

The Codes Of Hammurabi And Moses
W. W. Davies

QTY

The discovery of the Hammurabi Code is one of the greatest achievements of archaeology, and is of paramount interest, not only to the student of the Bible, but also to all those interested in ancient history...

Religion **ISBN:** *1-59462-338-4*   Pages:132
MSRP $12.95

The Theory of Moral Sentiments
Adam Smith

QTY

This work from 1749. contains original theories of conscience amd moral judgment and it is the foundation for systemof morals.

Philosophy ISBN: *1-59462-777-0*   Pages:536
MSRP $19.95

Jessica's First Prayer
Hesba Stretton

QTY

In a screened and secluded corner of one of the many railway-bridges which span the streets of London there could be seen a few years ago, from five o'clock every morning until half past eight, a tidily set-out coffee-stall, consisting of a trestle and board, upon which stood two large tin cans, with a small fire of charcoal burning under each so as to keep the coffee boiling during the early hours of the morning when the work-people were thronging into the city on their way to their daily toil...

Childrens   ISBN: *1-59462-373-2*   Pages:84
MSRP $9.95

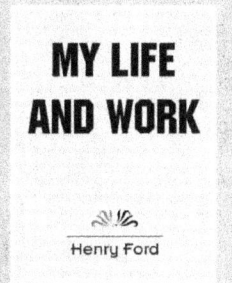

My Life and Work
Henry Ford

QTY

Henry Ford revolutionized the world with his implementation of mass production for the Model T automobile. Gain valuable business insight into his life and work with his own auto-biography... "We have only started on our development of our country we have not as yet, with all our talk of wonderful progress, done more than scratch the surface. The progress has been wonderful enough but..."

Biographies/ **ISBN:** *1-59462-198-5*   Pages:300
MSRP $21.95

www.bookjungle.com *email: sales@bookjungle.com fax: 630-214-0564 mail: Book Jungle PO Box 2226 Champaign, IL 61825*

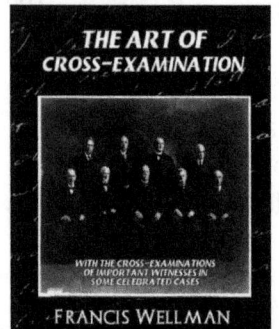

The Art of Cross-Examination
Francis Wellman

QTY

I presume it is the experience of every author, after his first book is published upon an important subject, to be almost overwhelmed with a wealth of ideas and illustrations which could readily have been included in his book, and which to his own mind, at least, seem to make a second edition inevitable. Such certainly was the case with me; and when the first edition had reached its sixth impression in five months, I rejoiced to learn that it seemed to my publishers that the book had met with a sufficiently favorable reception to justify a second and considerably enlarged edition. ..

Reference   ISBN: *1-59462-647-2*   Pages:412 MSRP *$19.95*

On the Duty of Civil Disobedience
Henry David Thoreau

QTY

Thoreau wrote his famous essay, On the Duty of Civil Disobedience, as a protest against an unjust but popular war and the immoral but popular institution of slave-owning. He did more than write—he declined to pay his taxes, and was hauled off to gaol in consequence. Who can say how much this refusal of his hastened the end of the war and of slavery ?

Law   ISBN: *1-59462-747-9*   Pages:48 MSRP *$7.45*

Dream Psychology Psychoanalysis for Beginners
Sigmund Freud

QTY

Sigmund Freud, born Sigismund Schlomo Freud (May 6, 1856 - September 23, 1939), was a Jewish-Austrian neurologist and psychiatrist who co-founded the psychoanalytic school of psychology. Freud is best known for his theories of the unconscious mind, especially involving the mechanism of repression; his redefinition of sexual desire as mobile and directed towards a wide variety of objects; and his therapeutic techniques, especially his understanding of transference in the therapeutic relationship and the presumed value of dreams as sources of insight into unconscious desires.

Psychology   ISBN: *1-59462-905-6*   Pages:196 MSRP *$15.45*

The Miracle of Right Thought
Orison Swett Marden

QTY

Believe with all of your heart that you will do what you were made to do. When the mind has once formed the habit of holding cheerful, happy, prosperous pictures, it will not be easy to form the opposite habit. It does not matter how improbable or how far away this realization may see, or how dark the prospects may be, if we visualize them as best we can, as vividly as possible, hold tenaciously to them and vigorously struggle to attain them, they will gradually become actualized, realized in the life. But a desire, a longing without endeavor, a yearning abandoned or held indifferently will vanish without realization.

Self Help   ISBN: *1-59462-644-8*   Pages:360 MSRP *$25.45*

www.bookjungle.com email: sales@bookjungle.com fax: 630-214-0564 mail: Book Jungle PO Box 2226 Champaign, IL 61825
QTY

| | **The Rosicrucian Cosmo-Conception Mystic Christianity** by *Max Heindel* | ISBN: *1-59462-188-8* | **$38.95** |

The Rosicrucian Cosmo-conception is not dogmatic, neither does it appeal to any other authority than the reason of the student. It is: not controversial, but is: sent forth in the, hope that it may help to clear...
New Age/Religion Pages 646

Abandonment To Divine Providence by *Jean-Pierre de Caussade* ISBN: *1-59462-228-0* **$25.95**
"The Rev. Jean Pierre de Caussade was one of the most remarkable spiritual writers of the Society of Jesus in France in the 18th Century. His death took place at Toulouse in 1751. His works have gone through many editions and have been republished...
Inspirational/Religion Pages 400

Mental Chemistry by *Charles Haanel* ISBN: *1-59462-192-6* **$23.95**
Mental Chemistry allows the change of material conditions by combining and appropriately utilizing the power of the mind. Much like applied chemistry creates something new and unique out of careful combinations of chemicals the mastery of mental chemistry...
New Age Pages 354

The Letters of Robert Browning and Elizabeth Barret Barrett 1845-1846 vol II ISBN: *1-59462-193-4* **$35.95**
by *Robert Browning* and *Elizabeth Barrett*
Biographies Pages 596

Gleanings In Genesis (volume I) by *Arthur W. Pink* ISBN: *1-59462-130-6* **$27.45**
Appropriately has Genesis been termed "the seed plot of the Bible" for in it we have, in germ form, almost all of the great doctrines which are afterwards fully developed in the books of Scripture which follow...
Religion/Inspirational Pages 420

The Master Key by *L. W. de Laurence* ISBN: *1-59462-001-6* **$30.95**
In no branch of human knowledge has there been a more lively increase of the spirit of research during the past few years than in the study of Psychology, Concentration and Mental Discipline. The requests for authentic lessons in Thought Control, Mental Discipline and...
New Age/Business Pages 422

The Lesser Key Of Solomon Goetia by *L. W. de Laurence* ISBN: *1-59462-092-X* **$9.95**
This translation of the first book of the "Lernegton" which is now for the first time made accessible to students of Talismanic Magic was done, after careful collation and edition, from numerous Ancient Manuscripts in Hebrew, Latin, and French...
New Age/Occult Pages 92

Rubaiyat Of Omar Khayyam by *Edward Fitzgerald* ISBN:*1-59462-332-5* **$13.95**
Edward Fitzgerald, whom the world has already learned, in spite of his own efforts to remain within the shadow of anonymity, to look upon as one of the rarest poets of the century, was born at Bredfield, in Suffolk, on the 31st of March, 1809. He was the third son of John Purcell...
Music Pages 172

Ancient Law by *Henry Maine* ISBN: *1-59462-128-4* **$29.95**
The chief object of the following pages is to indicate some of the earliest ideas of mankind, as they are reflected in Ancient Law, and to point out the relation of those ideas to modern thought.
Religion/History Pages 452

Far-Away Stories by *William J. Locke* ISBN: *1-59462-129-2* **$19.45**
"Good wine needs no bush, but a collection of mixed vintages does. And this book is just such a collection. Some of the stories I do not want to remain buried for ever in the museum files of dead magazine-numbers an author's not unpardonable vanity..."
Fiction Pages 272

Life of David Crockett by *David Crockett* ISBN: *1-59462-250-7* **$27.45**
"Colonel David Crockett was one of the most remarkable men of the times in which he lived. Born in humble life, but gifted with a strong will, an indomitable courage, and unremitting perseverance...
Biographies/New Age Pages 424

Lip-Reading by *Edward Nitchie* ISBN: *1-59462-206-X* **$25.95**
Edward B. Nitchie, founder of the New York School for the Hard of Hearing, now the Nitchie School of Lip-Reading, Inc, wrote "LIP-READING Principles and Practice". The development and perfecting of this meritorious work on lip-reading was an undertaking...
How-to Pages 400

A Handbook of Suggestive Therapeutics, Applied Hypnotism, Psychic Science ISBN: *1-59462-214-0* **$24.95**
by *Henry Munro*
Health/New Age/Health/Self-help Pages 376

A Doll's House: and Two Other Plays by *Henrik Ibsen* ISBN: *1-59462-112-8* **$19.95**
Henrik Ibsen created this classic when in revolutionary 1848 Rome. Introducing some striking concepts in playwriting for the realist genre, this play has been studied the world over.
Fiction/Classics/Plays 308

The Light of Asia by *sir Edwin Arnold* ISBN: *1-59462-204-3* **$13.95**
In this poetic masterpiece, Edwin Arnold describes the life and teachings of Buddha. The man who was to become known as Buddha to the world was born as Prince Gautama of India but he rejected the worldly riches and abandoned the reigns of power when...
Religion/History/Biographies Pages 170

The Complete Works of Guy de Maupassant by *Guy de Maupassant* ISBN: *1-59462-157-8* **$16.95**
"For days and days, nights and nights, I had dreamed of that first kiss which was to consecrate our engagement, and I knew not on what spot I should put my lips..."
Fiction/Classics Pages 240

The Art of Cross-Examination by *Francis L. Wellman* ISBN: *1-59462-309-0* **$26.95**
Written by a renowned trial lawyer, Wellman imparts his experience and uses case studies to explain how to use psychology to extract desired information through questioning.
How-to/Science/Reference Pages 408

Answered or Unanswered? by *Louisa Vaughan* ISBN: *1-59462-248-5* **$10.95**
Miracles of Faith in China
Religion Pages 112

The Edinburgh Lectures on Mental Science (1909) by *Thomas* ISBN: *1-59462-008-3* **$11.95**
This book contains the substance of a course of lectures recently given by the writer in the Queen Street Hall, Edinburgh. Its purpose is to indicate the Natural Principles governing the relation between Mental Action and Material Conditions...
New Age/Psychology Pages 148

Ayesha by *H. Rider Haggard* ISBN: *1-59462-301-5* **$24.95**
Verily and indeed it is the unexpected that happens! Probably if there was one person upon the earth from whom the Editor of this, and of a certain previous history, did not expect to hear again...
Classics Pages 380

Ayala's Angel by *Anthony Trollope* ISBN: *1-59462-352-X* **$29.95**
The two girls were both pretty, but Lucy who was twenty-one who supposed to be simple and comparatively unattractive, whereas Ayala was credited, as her Bombwhat romantic name might show, with poetic charm and a taste for romance. Ayala when her father died was nineteen...
Fiction Pages 484

The American Commonwealth by *James Bryce* ISBN: *1-59462-286-8* **$34.45**
An interpretation of American democratic political theory. It examines political mechanics and society from the perspective of Scotsman James Bryce
Politics Pages 572

Stories of the Pilgrims by *Margaret P. Pumphrey* ISBN: *1-59462-116-0* **$17.95**
This book explores pilgrims religious oppression in England as well as their escape to Holland and eventual crossing to America on the Mayflower, and their early days in New England...
History Pages 268

www.bookjungle.com email: sales@bookjungle.com fax: 630-214-0564 mail: Book Jungle PO Box 2226 Champaign, IL 61825

QTY

The Fasting Cure by *Sinclair Upton* ISBN: *1-59462-222-1* **$13.95**
In the Cosmopolitan Magazine for May, 1910, and in the Contemporary Review (London) for April, 1910, I published an article dealing with my experiences in fasting. I have written a great many magazine articles, but never one which attracted so much attention... New Age/Self Help/Health Pages 164

Hebrew Astrology by *Sepharial* ISBN: *1-59462-308-2* **$13.45**
In these days of advanced thinking it is a matter of common observation that we have left many of the old landmarks behind and that we are now pressing forward to greater heights and to a wider horizon than that which represented the mind-content of our progenitors... Astrology Pages 144

Thought Vibration or The Law of Attraction in the Thought World ISBN: *1-59462-127-6* **$12.95**
by *William Walker Atkinson* Psychology/Religion Pages 144

Optimism by *Helen Keller* ISBN: *1-59462-108-X* **$15.95**
Helen Keller was blind, deaf, and mute since 19 months old, yet famously learned how to overcome these handicaps, communicate with the world, and spread her lectures promoting optimism. An inspiring read for everyone... Biographies/Inspirational Pages 84

Sara Crewe by *Frances Burnett* ISBN: *1-59462-360-0* **$9.45**
In the first place, Miss Minchin lived in London. Her home was a large, dull, tall one, in a large, dull square, where all the houses were alike, and all the sparrows were alike, and where all the door-knockers made the same heavy sound... Childrens/Classic Pages 88

The Autobiography of Benjamin Franklin by *Benjamin Franklin* ISBN: *1-59462-135-7* **$24.95**
The Autobiography of Benjamin Franklin has probably been more extensively read than any other American historical work, and no other book of its kind has had such ups and downs of fortune. Franklin lived for many years in England, where he was agent... Biographies/History Pages 332

Name	
Email	
Telephone	
Address	
City, State ZIP	

☐ Credit Card   ☐ Check / Money Order

Credit Card Number	
Expiration Date	
Signature	

Please Mail to: Book Jungle
PO Box 2226
Champaign, IL 61825
or Fax to: 630-214-0564

ORDERING INFORMATION

web: *www.bookjungle.com*
email: *sales@bookjungle.com*
fax: *630-214-0564*
mail: *Book Jungle PO Box 2226 Champaign, IL 61825*
or PayPal *to sales@bookjungle.com*

Please contact us for bulk discounts

DIRECT-ORDER TERMS

**20% Discount if You Order
Two or More Books**
Free Domestic Shipping!
Accepted: Master Card, Visa,
Discover, American Express

www.ingramcontent.com/pod-product-compliance
Lightning Source LLC
Chambersburg PA
CBHW081325040426
42453CB00013B/2301